Fetch!

PUGS

Kate Riggs

Creative Education · Creative Paperbacks

published by Creative Education and Creative Paperbacks
P.O. Box 227, Mankato, Minnesota 56002
Creative Education and Creative Paperbacks are imprints of
The Creative Company
www.thecreativecompany.us

design and production by Christine Vanderbeek
art direction by Rita Marshall
printed in the United States of America

photographs by Alamy (blickwinkel; Everett Collection,
Inc.; Tierfotoagentur; United Archives GmbH), Dreamstime
(Kitchner Bain, Chris Lorenz, Putnik), iStockphoto
(baratroli, GlobalP, rusm, Suzifoo, utkamandarinka),
Shutterstock (5 second Studio, Utekhina Anna, Aseph,
gp88, Wasitt Hemwarapornchai, Pavel Hlystov, Eric
Isselee, Neveshkin Nikolay, Oleg_Mit, Valerio Pardi,
Roman Prishenko, Scorpp, Viorel Sima, Nikolai Tsvetkov,
WilleeCole Photography)

library of congress cataloging-in-publication data
Names: Riggs, Kate, author.
Title: Pugs / Kate Riggs.
Series: Fetch!
Includes bibliographical references and index.
Summary: A brief overview of the physical characteristics,
personality traits, and habits of the pug breed, as well as
descriptions of famous pop-culture pugs such as Frank.
Identifiers:
ISBN 978-1-60818-900-7 (hardcover)
ISBN 978-1-62832-516-4 (pbk)
ISBN 978-1-56660-952-4 (eBook)
This title has been submitted for CIP processing under
LCCN 2017938926.
CCSS: RI.1.1, 2, 4, 5, 6, 7; RI.2.1, 2, 5, 6, 7;
RI.3.1, 5, 7; RF.1.1, 3, 4; RF.2.3, 4

first edition HC 9 8 7 6 5 4 3 2 1
first edition PBK 9 8 7 6 5 4 3 2 1

TABLE OF CONTENTS

LOVING PUGS

A pug is a *breed* of dog. Pugs love
to be loved. They get lonely easily.
So they will follow their people every-
where! Any lap makes a good seat.

WHAT DO PUGS LOOK LIKE?

Pugs are small dogs with curly tails. Their faces have deep wrinkles. They are known for their smashed-in *muzzles*. A pug's flat face means it cannot breathe as easily as other dogs. Many pugs snort and snore loudly.

A pug's short body usually has some wrinkles and rolls.

Fetch!

Fawn pugs are a light tan color. Pugs can also be black or *brindle*. Their fur is short. Many pugs have square bodies. They weigh about 14 to 18 pounds (6.4–8.2 kg). Longer, taller pugs can weigh more.

PUG PUPPIES

Tiny pug puppies weigh about four pounds (1.8 kg) by eight weeks of age. This is usually when they leave their mother. Pug puppies like to play with toys. They pounce and "play bow."

Young pug puppies sleep up to 20 hours a day.

PUGS ON THE SCREEN

Pugs have starred in lots of movies. *The Adventures of Milo and Otis* (1989) is about a pug, Otis, and his tabby-cat best friend. In 2016, a pug named Mel was featured in *The Secret Life of Pets*. Mel joins his friends on a rescue mission across New York City.

When Milo and Otis get separated, they set out to find each other.

PUGS AND PEOPLE

Pugs came from China and Tibet hundreds of years ago. They became popular with *royal* families around the world. Pugs have always been people-pleasers. They make excellent family dogs. Their owners need to take good care of them.

Adult pugs are 10 to 14 inches (25.4–35.6 cm) tall.

The wrinkles on a pug's face need to be cleaned often. Dirt can collect around the nose and eyes. The pug's eyes stick out from its head. Pug owners must watch out for things that can poke the eyes.

Pugs should be brushed and their wrinkles cleaned weekly.

Fetch!

WHAT DO PUGS LIKE TO DO?

Pugs love to spend time with people. Pugs of all ages like to snuggle. Young pugs like to exercise. But pugs can overheat easily. Help your pug stay safe on hot days.

Easy-going pugs play well with children and other animals.

Pugs want to go where you go. They want to do what you do. Go for a walk. Then sit in the shade. Your pug will lie in the grass next to you—unless he is sitting on your lap!

A FAMOUS PUG

Frank is a talking pug from the movies
Men in Black (1997) and *Men in Black II*
(2002). He looks like a normal pug, but he
is really an alien! He helps **agents** called
the Men in Black. (These secret agents look
after aliens living on Earth.) In the second
movie, Frank works for the Men in Black.
Then he is known as "Agent F."

GLOSSARY

agents people who work for the government or other organizations

breed a kind of an animal with certain traits, such as long ears or a good nose

brindle a brown or yellowish-brown color, with streaks of other colors

muzzles the nose and mouth of some animals, such as dogs

royal belonging to a king or queen's family

READ MORE

Bozzo, Linda. *I Like Pugs!* New York: Enslow, 2017.

Heos, Bridget. *Do You Really Want a Dog?* North Mankato, Minn.: Amicus, 2014.

Wendorff, Anne. *Pugs*. Minneapolis: Bellwether Media, 2010.

WEBSITES

American Kennel Club: Pug
http://www.akc.org/dog-breeds/pug/
Learn more about pugs, and check out lots of pug pictures.

Bailey's Responsible Dog Owner's Coloring Book
http://classic.akc.org/pdfs/public_education/coloring_book.pdf
Print out pictures to color, and learn more about caring for a pet dog.

Every effort has been made to ensure that these sites are suitable for children, that they have educational value, and that they contain no inappropriate material. However, because of the nature of the Internet, it is impossible to guarantee that these sites will remain active indefinitely or that their contents will not be altered.

INDEX